ANIMAL BATTLES

# CANADA GOOSE VS. GRAY FOX

BY NATHAN SOMMER

TORQUE, AN IMPRINT OF BELLWETHER MEDIA BY FLUTTERBEE

**Torque** brims with excitement perfect for thrill-seekers of all kinds. Discover daring survival skills, explore uncharted worlds, and marvel at mighty engines and extreme sports. In *Torque* books, anything can happen. Are you ready?

This edition first published in 2026 by Bellwether Media, Inc.



For information regarding permission, write to Bellwether Media, Inc., Attention: Permissions Department, 3500 American Blvd W, Suite 150, Bloomington, MN 55431.

Library of Congress Cataloging-in-Publication Data is available at www.loc.gov or upon request from the publisher.

ISBN: 9798893048339 (hardcover)
ISBN: 9798898800130 (paperback)
ISBN: 9798893049336 (ebook)

Editor: Suzane Nguyen Designer: Josh Brink Series Designer: Andrea Schneider

Printed in the United States of America, North Mankato, MN.

# TABLE OF CONTENTS

# THE COMPETITORS

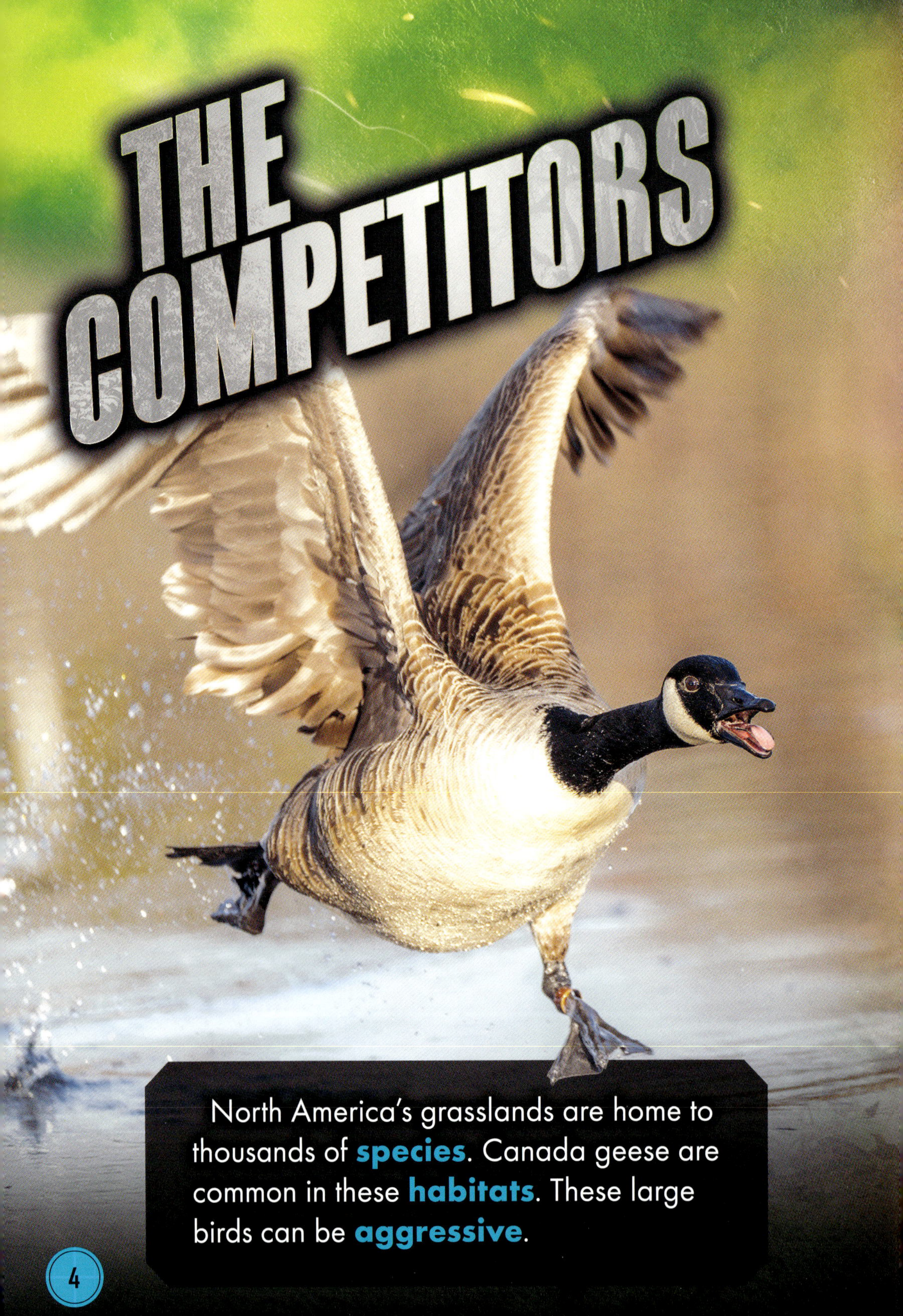

North America's grasslands are home to thousands of **species**. Canada geese are common in these **habitats**. These large birds can be **aggressive**.

Geese share some habitats with gray foxes. The foxes climb and pounce to hunt their meals. Who wins when these two animals come face-to-face?

# CANADA GOOSE PROFILE

**WEIGHT**

AROUND 20 POUNDS (9 KILOGRAMS)

**LENGTH**

3.6 FEET (1.1 METERS)

**WINGSPAN**

OVER 6 FEET (1.8 METERS)

**HABITATS**

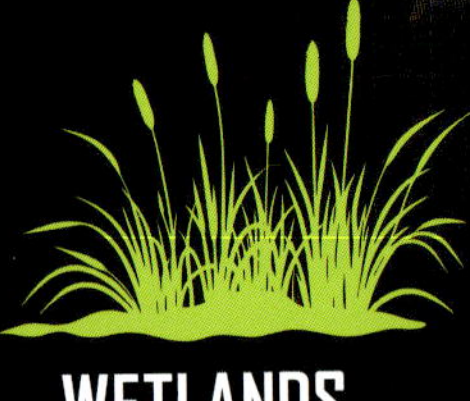

WETLANDS

GRASSLANDS

**CANADA GOOSE RANGE**

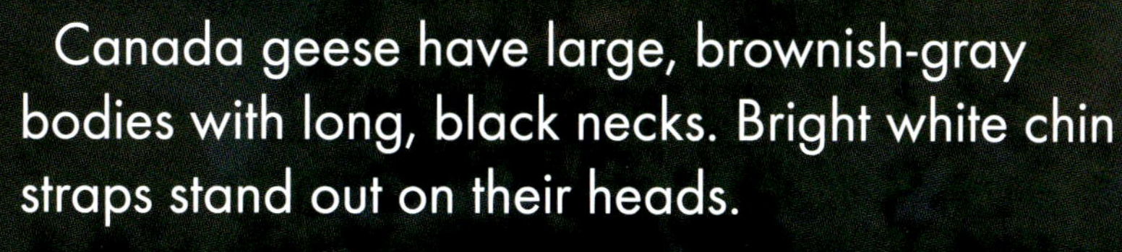

Canada geese have large, brownish-gray bodies with long, black necks. Bright white chin straps stand out on their heads.

Canada geese are found throughout the United States and Canada. Some **migrate** to northern Mexico during the winter. They live in flocks that can have thousands of members.

**GOING THE DISTANCE**

**Canada geese can fly up to 1,500 miles (2,414 kilometers) in one day.**

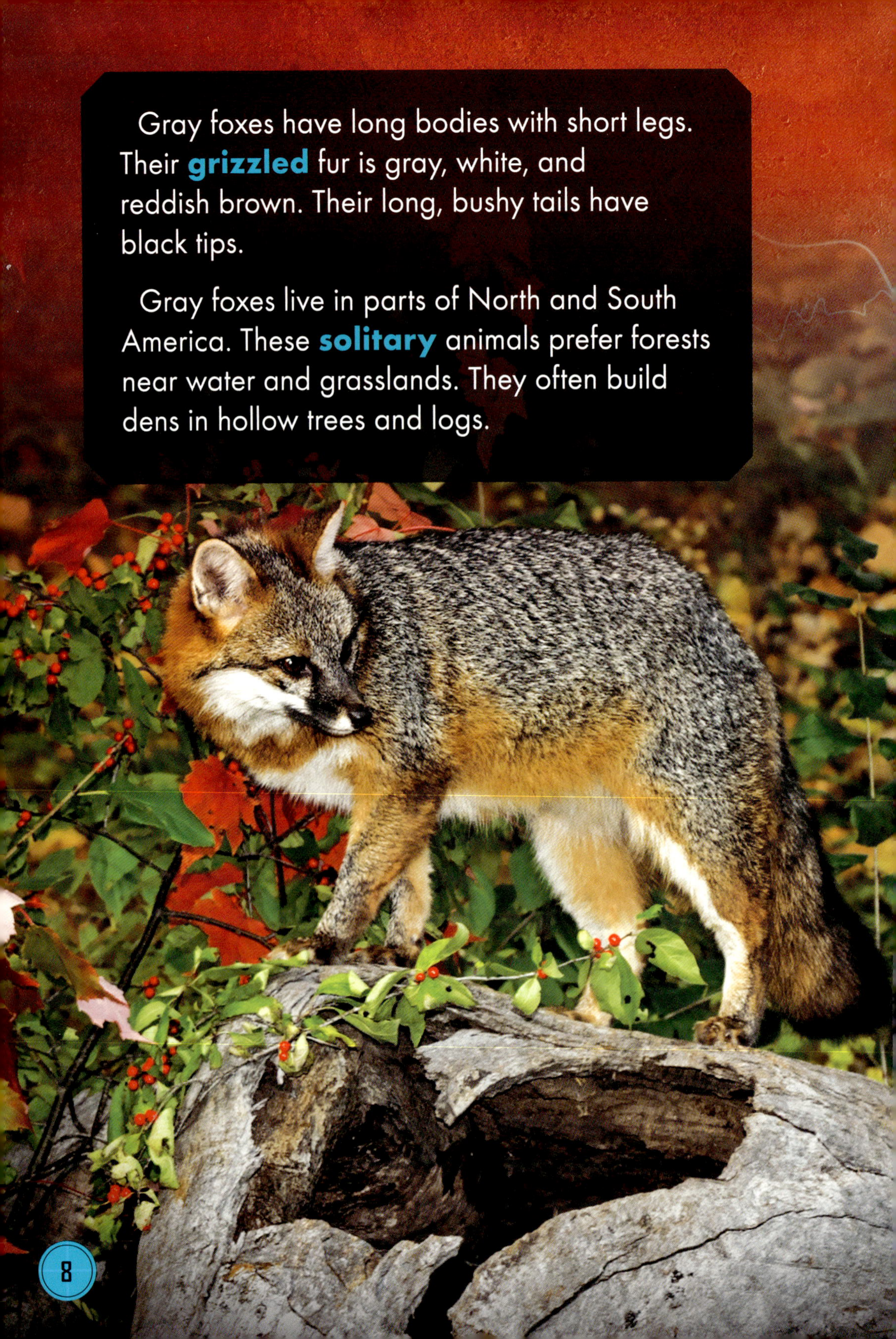

Gray foxes have long bodies with short legs. Their **grizzled** fur is gray, white, and reddish brown. Their long, bushy tails have black tips.

Gray foxes live in parts of North and South America. These **solitary** animals prefer forests near water and grasslands. They often build dens in hollow trees and logs.

# GRAY FOX PROFILE

**LENGTH**

UP TO 3.6 FEET (1.1 METERS) INCLUDING TAIL

**WEIGHT**

UP TO 19.8 POUNDS (9 KILOGRAMS)

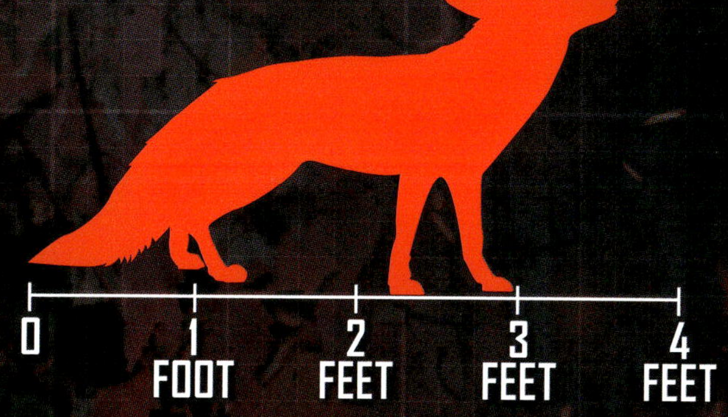


**HABITATS**

FORESTS

GRASSLANDS

FARMLANDS

**GRAY FOX RANGE**

# SECRET WEAPONS

Gray foxes are excellent climbers. They have **semi-retractable claws** that easily hold onto trees. They quickly climb trees to hunt **prey** and escape from danger.

## CANINE CLIMBERS

Gray foxes are the only foxes in North America that can climb trees.

# SIZE COMPARISON

The largest Canada geese have a wingspan of over 6 feet (1.8 meters). Their wings help them fly at speeds around 40 miles (64 kilometers) per hour. The birds can fly long distances quickly.

# SECRET WEAPONS

CANADA GOOSE

LARGE WINGSPAN

LARGE WEBBED FEET

POWERFUL BEAK

Large webbed feet make Canada geese excellent swimmers. Their feet help **propel** the birds through water. They can speedily swim away to avoid enemies.

GRAY FOX

# SECRET WEAPONS

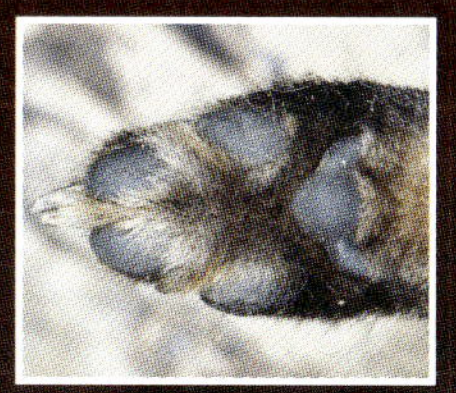
SEMI-RETRACTABLE CLAWS

LARGE, POINTED EARS

STRONG LEGS

Gray foxes have great hearing. Their large, pointed ears can hear prey hidden underground or beneath snow. This helps them know exactly where to pounce!

Canada geese have powerful beaks with **serrated** edges. The beaks can tear apart tough grass. The birds also use their beaks to strike and bite enemies.

28 MILES (45 KILOMETERS) PER HOUR

GRAY FOX

28 MILES (45 KILOMETERS) PER HOUR

FASTEST HUMAN

Gray fox legs are short but strong. They use these to easily jump between tree branches. The foxes are also fast. They can reach speeds of up to 28 miles (45 kilometers) per hour.

# ATTACK MOVES

Canada geese are aggressive when protecting their young. The birds stretch their necks and hiss as a warning. They also spread their wings. If this does not work, they charge!

Gray foxes are **opportunistic** hunters. They use super senses to smell and hear prey. Then they pounce feet first to **ambush** it!

## GRAY FOX DIET

Gray foxes mostly hunt mice and birds. They also eat fruit and seeds.

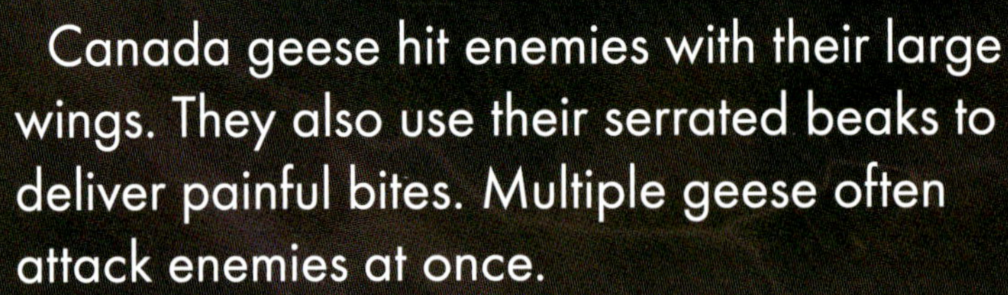

Canada geese hit enemies with their large wings. They also use their serrated beaks to deliver painful bites. Multiple geese often attack enemies at once.

## POWERFUL STRIKES

**Strikes from Canada geese wings can knock over an adult human.**

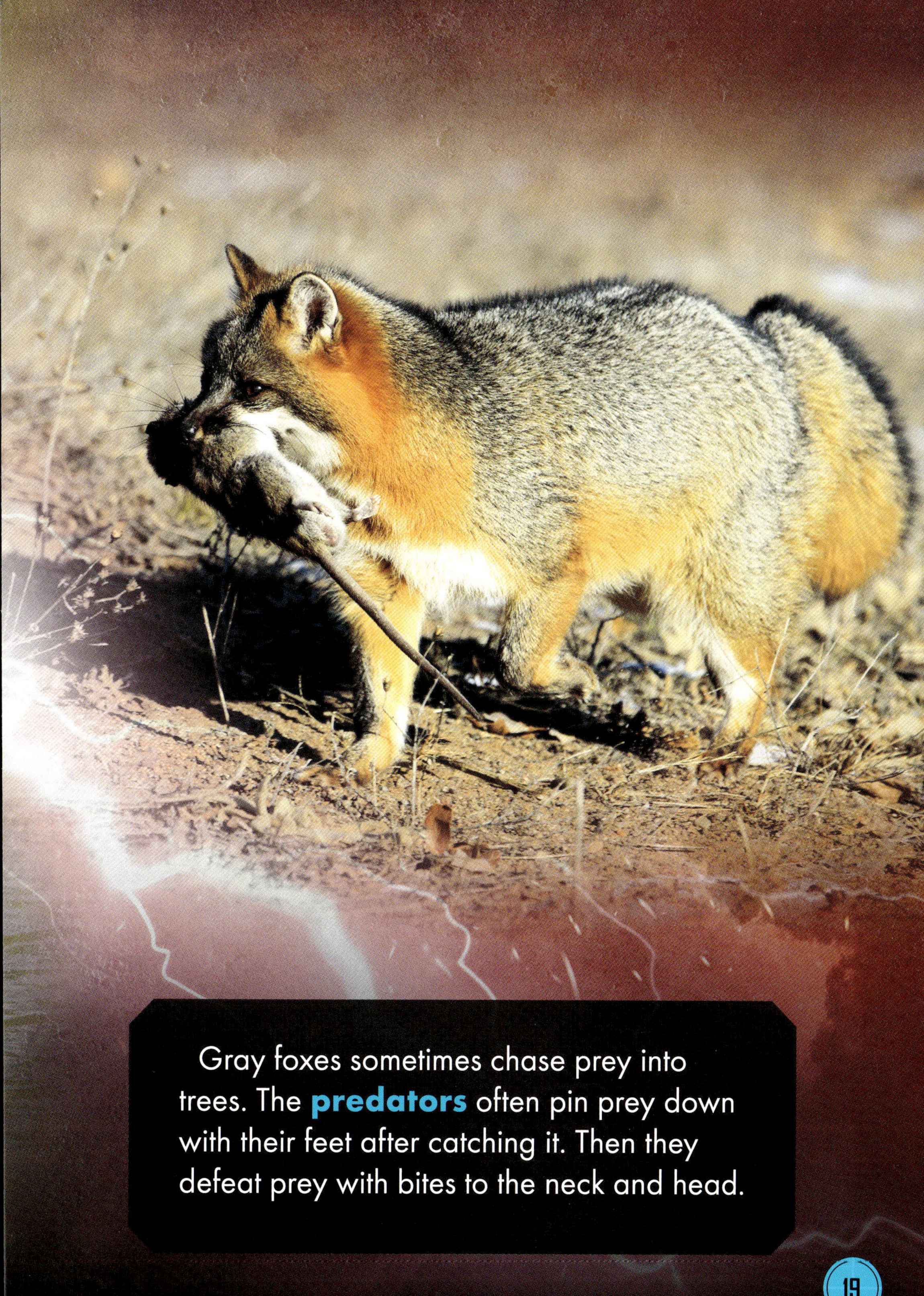

Gray foxes sometimes chase prey into trees. The **predators** often pin prey down with their feet after catching it. Then they defeat prey with bites to the neck and head.

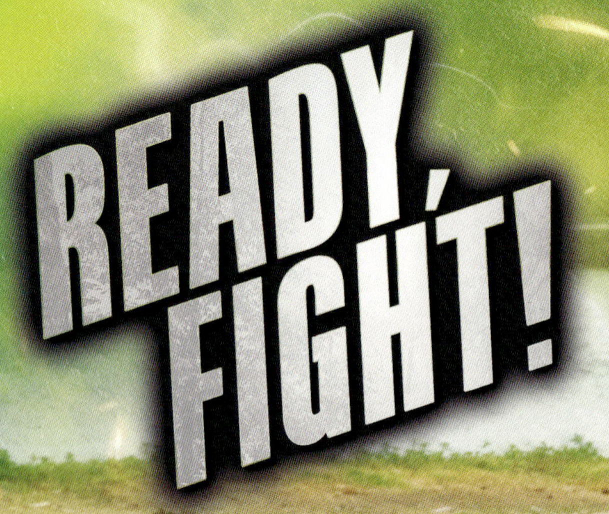


A gray fox hears a baby Canada goose. It waits to ambush and pounce on the baby. Suddenly, the fox is knocked over by the mother goose's wings!

The fox jumps on the mother goose. But the goose escapes its grip. The goose strikes and bites until the fox runs up a tree. The goose protected its young today!

# GLOSSARY

**aggressive**—ready to fight

**ambush**—to carry out a surprise attack

**grizzled**—streaked with gray

**habitats**—the homes or areas where animals prefer to live

**migrate**—to travel from one place to another, often with the seasons

**opportunistic**—taking advantage of a situation

**predators**—animals that hunt other animals for food

**prey**—animals that are hunted by other animals for food

**propel**—to push forward

**semi-retractable claws**—claws that are out and visible at all times

**serrated**—having a blade like that of a saw

**solitary**—living alone

**species**—kinds of animals

# TO LEARN MORE

## AT THE LIBRARY

Emminizer, Theresa. *Bird Life Cycles.* Buffalo, N.Y.: Enslow Publishing, 2025.

O'Brien, Cynthia. *Arctic Fox vs. Red Fox.* Minneapolis, Minn.: Kaleidoscope, 2025.

Sommer, Nathan. *Arctic Fox vs. Snowy Owl.* Minneapolis, Minn.: Bellwether Media, 2024.

## ON THE WEB

**FACTSURFER**

Factsurfer.com gives you a safe, fun way to find more information.

1. Go to www.factsurfer.com
2. Enter "Canada goose vs. gray fox" into the search box and click 🔍.
3. Select your book cover to see a list of related content.

# INDEX



The images in this book are reproduced through the courtesy of: Mark, front cover (Canada Goose); ranchorunner, front cover (gray fox), p. 12 (large wingspan); David A Litman, pp. 2-3 (background), 20-24 (background); MrWildLife, pp. 2-3 (goose), 20-24 (goose); geoffkuchera, pp. 2-3 (fox), 20-24 (fox); Cami Johnson, pp. 4, 12 (powerful beak); Holly Kuchera, p. 5; 925am, pp. 6-7; PaoloBrt, p. 7 (goose vector); Geoffrey Kuchera, pp. 8-9; M Sohail12345, p. 9 (fox vector); hkuchera, p. 10; Denny, p. 11; GKProStudio, p. 11 (goose vector); JT8, p. 12 (large, webbed feet); Mike, p. 12; JOHN M. COFFMAN/ Science Photo Library, p. 13 (semi-retractable claws); Travis Potter, p. 13 (large, pointed ears & strong legs); Tom Walker/ Getty Images, p. 13; Paul Binet, p. 14; Warren Metcalf, p. 15; Jason Kostansek, p. 16; Travis, p. 17; Ian Duffield, p. 18; Mikael Males, p. 19.